PEOPLE OF PEACE

BY ROSE BLUE AND
CORINNE J. NADEN

The Millbrook Press, Brookfield, Connecticut

Cover photos all courtesy of Bettmann except Jane Addams,
courtesy of National Portrait Gallery, Art Resource, NY.

All photos courtesy of Bettmann except pp. 51, 69,
courtesy of AP/Wide World.

Library of Congress Cataloging-in-Publication Data
Blue, Rose.
People of peace/by Rose Blue and Corinne J. Naden.
p.   cm.
Includes bibliographical references and index.
Summary: Eleven people who have worked to promote peace,
within their countries or internationally, are profiled.
Subjects include India's Mohandas Gandhi, South Africa's
Desmond Tutu, America's Jane Addams and Jimmy Carter, and
other historical and contemporary leaders.
ISBN 1-56294-409-6 (lib. bdg.)
1. Pacifists—Biography—Juvenile literature. 2. Peace—
Juvenile literature.   I. Naden, Corinne J.   II. Title.
JX1962.A2B58   1994   327.1'72'0922—dc20
[B]   93-30547   CIP   AC

Published by The Millbrook Press
2 Old New Milford Road, Brookfield, Connecticut 06804

CONTENTS

PEOPLE OF PEACE

INTRODUCTION

Peace. The word means "freedom from confusion," a condition of "public quiet." It has been used as a greeting of goodwill in all countries of the world and throughout all centuries. People wish for "peace on earth" each time the Christmas bells ring. *Shalom*, the Hebrew word for peace, is spoken by Jews after every Sabbath service.

To most people, however, *peace* simply means "no war." Unfortunately, history records very few times of "no war" anywhere in the world. One war ends and another begins. World War II ended in the 1940s, and the war in Korea began in the 1950s. The threat of nuclear war faded somewhat with the collapse of the Soviet Union as the 1990s began. But there was the Persian Gulf War in early 1991 and fighting in the former Yugoslavia in 1993 . . . and on and on.

Most people wish for peace in the world. Wishing, alas, doesn't make it so. Some people actually work for peace. They devote most or much of their lives to help bring peace to the world or to their own particular part of it. The search for peace has been going on for centuries. It goes back to the very earliest of recorded times. It goes back, more recently, to the Congress of Vienna in 1815 when European leaders met to establish peace after the overthrow of Napoleon. It goes back to the League of Nations in the years after World War I and to the United Nations in the years after World War II. Both organizations were established in the hope that if people have a place to talk, they won't fight.

The League of Nations (1920–1946), fought for so strenuously by President Woodrow Wilson, was organized after World War I to solve conflicts peacefully. Unfortunately, its influence was minimal, partly because the United States never signed the treaty that established the League.

The United Nations grew out of a 1945 conference in San Francisco, where fifty countries signed the UN Charter on October 24. Headquartered in four buildings on the East River in New York City, the UN is dedicated to keeping peace throughout the world, to developing friendly relations among nations, to working together to better the lives of the poor, the sick, the illiterate, and to being a center that helps all nations to achieve these goals.

Men and women, rich and poor, from all countries have joined in the search for peace in the world. American businessman Henry Ford guided a party to Europe to organize a conference to end World War I. In 1915 he set sail on a vessel he named the *Peace Ship*. Robert Cecil, a member of the British Parliament, helped to draft the League of Nations covenant. Mother Teresa of India has tirelessly traveled the world to bring peace and comfort to the desperately poor. Kurt Mazur, a German conductor now with New York City's Philharmonic Orchestra, called for the tearing down of the Berlin Wall in the 1980s.

Some of the people who work for peace have received the Nobel Peace Prize. The prize may be awarded each year to a person, institution, or association recognized as having done the most to bring about peace in the world. It is the only one of the six Nobel prizes awarded from Oslo, Norway. The other prizes—which are for physics, chemistry, physiology or medicine, literature, and economics—are given out in Stockholm, Sweden. Stockholm was the birthplace of Alfred Nobel in 1833. By the time of his death in 1896, this scientist and inventor had amassed a large fortune. It may be hard to believe, but most of his money had come from his inventions of dynamite and other explosives. As though to atone for the destruction his genius created, he left his millions to those who worked for people and for peace.

There are many members of the mighty "peace army." The eleven men and women singled out in this book are only a few. They were selected because they have done outstanding work for peace and because their lives show that peace seekers, past and present, come from different walks of life and different places in the world. The peace workers in this book happen to be from the United States, India, Sweden, South Africa, Costa Rica, and Northern Ireland. But others have been, and are, from anywhere.

Despite the work of many, the quest for a way to end war is far from over. As we approach the twenty-first century, we salute those who are still searching.

Let us meet these People of Peace.

Andrew Carnegie devoted much of the fortune he made in industry to the cause of world peace.

ANDREW CARNEGIE
(1835-1919)

AMERICAN INDUSTRIALIST
AND PHILANTHROPIST

**Since 1910 the Carnegie Endowment
has kept alive the belief of this U.S.
industrialist that his wealth and
power could advance the cause
of world peace.**

Andrew Carnegie first saw the United States at the age of twelve. He was born in Scotland, at Dunfermline, Fife, on November 25, 1835. By the time of his death nearly eighty-four years later, he was a millionaire many times over. He had sparked the expansion of the U.S. steel industry through the nineteenth century and was looked on as one of the great philanthropists of his era.

Carnegie became one of the world's richest and best-known figures. Less well known was his deep belief that his power and wealth could best be used in the cause of world peace. "Those who are blessed with wealth have a duty to give back to society," he said.

This self-made millionaire was certainly not blessed with wealth at the beginning of his life. His father was a poor weaver who moved his family to the United States in 1848. The Carnegies settled in Allegheny, now part of Pittsburgh, Pennsylvania. While still a teen-ager, Andrew got his first job in a cotton factory and then became a telegraph messenger and operator for the Pennsylvania Railroad Company.

His keen mind and good work habits eventually drew the attention of the company president, Thomas Scott. Young Carnegie became Scott's personal secretary in 1853. Six years later he was superintendent of the company's western division. In that job he introduced sleeping cars to the railroad.

Although he was devoted to his duties, Carnegie had his eye on the future as well. He carefully invested his earnings in various industrial and financial enterprises. By the time he was thirty years old, in 1865, his annual income had reached $50,000, an enormous sum at that time.

Carnegie left the Pennsylvania Railroad Company the year he was thirty and became manager of the Keystone Bridge Company. Within a few years his concentration was almost totally on steel. To Carnegie, the future of U.S. industry rested in what he believed would be a huge and growing demand for iron and steel. In 1872 he founded what later became the Carnegie Steel Company.

During that decade, Carnegie Steel built the first U.S. steel plants to use the Bessemer process. Englishman Henry Bessemer had invented a way of speeding up the slow, costly, and cumbersome production of steel. Carnegie thought it looked promising. Any new method that seemed workable, even if untried, often caught his attention. Under his leadership Carnegie Steel was willing to test the latest innovations. In a few years Carnegie would drop the Bessemer process for the open-hearth furnace, which produced purer steel at a faster, more efficient rate than did the Bessemer process. The open-hearth furnace accounted for most of the steel made in the twentieth century. Today, however, most steel is manufactured by an even more efficient method known as the oxygen process.

Busy as he was, Andrew Carnegie found time for more in his life than steel. In 1887, at the age of fifty-two, he was wedded to Louise Whitfield of New York, and they remained happily married until his death. The Carnegies had one daughter, Margaret.

By 1890 the success of Carnegie Steel was a large part of the reason that the United States, for the first time, produced more steel than Great Britain. Carnegie's company continued to prosper, but in 1901 he decided to retire. He sold his company to the United States

Steel Corporation and received $250 million for his share in it. It was said that after the sale, J. P. Morgan, who owned U.S. Steel, traveled to Carnegie's mansion on East Ninety-first Street in New York City and congratulated him on becoming the richest man in the world.

Now the richest man in the world could concentrate on using his wealth to help people and to bring peace in the world.

Andrew Carnegie was a self-made man, a self-educated man, intelligent and shrewd when he had to be, gentle and charming when he wished. His ego and self-confidence were huge. Many said he was ruthless in his business dealings. His curiosity was boundless. Yet for all his riches and power, he rarely displayed his wealth on the grand scale of so many tycoons of his day and the present. In fact, Carnegie vowed that he would give away most of his fortune during his lifetime. After he retired, he set about doing just that.

His gift-giving is legendary. He founded the Carnegie Institute of Technology at Carnegie-Mellon University in Pittsburgh in 1900 and the Carnegie Institution in Washington, D.C., in 1902. He gave large sums of money to Tuskegee Institute, founded in 1881 by black American educator Booker T. Washington in Tuskegee, Alabama. He set up a pension fund for college professors in America through the Carnegie Foundation for the Advancement of Teachers in New York City in 1905. He gave money to establish many libraries in the United States, Great Britain, and other countries.

He also built Carnegie Hall, the historic concert hall in New York City named for him. Since its opening in May 1891, Carnegie Hall has been the stage for nearly every important American and foreign musician in the world. Although it is no longer home to the New York Philharmonic Orchestra, which moved to New York's vast music-theater-dance complex, Lincoln Center, in the 1960s, the name of this concert hall is still magic. From Peter Ilich Tchaikovsky, who was guest conductor during its opening week, to Frank Sinatra, any musician will tell you that you haven't made it until you've played Carnegie Hall. The hall was renovated in 1986 and continues to operate in historic splendor.

Carnegie made headlines all of his adult life with his many philanthropic gestures. One of the biggest came in 1910: "Andrew

Carnegie Gives Ten Millions to Promote Peace Throughout the World." And so, the Carnegie Endowment for International Peace came into being.

The main goal of the Carnegie Endowment for International Peace is the prevention of war. The Carnegie Endowment employs people with many backgrounds and interests. They try to form policies that will influence governments and nations on such topics as U.S.-Russian relations or stopping the spread of nuclear weapons. They hold conferences and programs in New York City and all around the world to talk about policies that will strengthen peace. They promote study groups to find ways to settle differences among people and nations. The Endowment publishes a journal each quarter, called *Foreign Policy*, in which it discusses and promotes ideas for peaceful solutions to problems.

Why did Carnegie wait until 1910 to establish this organization? He said he had never felt that the time was right. And as much as any other factor, a speech by President William Howard Taft pushed him into setting up the organization. Carnegie had been lukewarm about Taft until the President spoke at the Hotel Astor in New York City on March 22, 1910. Taft discussed his belief that matters of national honor should be referred to a court of arbitration. Carnegie saw this as a means to avert wars. It propelled him into the action that led to the Carnegie Endowment.

The first president of the Carnegie organization was Elihu Root, who had served as U.S. secretary of state from 1905 to 1909. Root won the 1912 Nobel Peace Prize. He continued as president of the Carnegie Endowment until 1925 and remained a trusted adviser to Carnegie. Carnegie's wife, Louise, once told Root that he understood her husband "better than anyone else."

After Carnegie's work in establishing the foundation and the gift of millions, he was bitterly disappointed at the outbreak of World War I in 1914. He said, "All my air castles have fallen about me like a house of cards." The war years were a time of deep sadness for him. Although in failing health, he lived long enough to rejoice in the armistice that ended the war in 1918. Andrew Carnegie died a year later, on August 11, 1919, in Lenox, Massachusetts.

Was Andrew Carnegie a naïve dreamer? Surely, his search for peace in the world has not succeeded. But although the dream remains a dream, Carnegie's search goes on through the work of the many institutions that bear his name. The Carnegie Endowment continues to serve as a think tank that seeks peaceful solutions to international differences both in the present and the future.

Carnegie's dream also continues in the Carnegie Council, now known as the Carnegie Council on Ethics and International Affairs, which he established with $2 million. He felt that religious leaders should and could unite in the monumental task of finding world peace. When he called the original trustees of the Council together in his living room in New York City in 1914, Carnegie told them: "No less than twelve of the chief religious bodies of the civilized world [are] here represented by their prominent official leaders . . . to cooperate as one body in the holy task of abolishing war." Today, the Council carries on in Carnegie's name. By its programs, forums, and publications, the Council, although recognizing the long journey still ahead, continues Andrew Carnegie's search for a "pattern for peace."

Best known for her work as a social reformer, Jane Addams was also a leader in the struggle to prevent war.

JANE ADDAMS
(1860-1935)

AMERICAN SOCIAL WORKER
AND PACIFIST; WINNER,
1931 NOBEL PEACE PRIZE

A dedicated seeker of world peace and advocate for women's rights, Addams is best remembered as the founder of Hull House, one of the first social settlements in North America.

The eighth and last child of Sarah and John Addams was a daughter named Laura Jane. She was born on September 6, 1860, in Cedarville, Illinois, 80 miles (130 kilometers) west of Chicago. But Cedarville might as well have been the moon; it was that different from the Chicago slums where Jane Addams would spend most of her adult life. She was born into a family of means. Her father was a state senator, a banker, and a mill owner. He was also a Quaker, a member of a religion devoted to peace. Jane's mother died before she was three years old.

Most women at that time did not have a career outside the home. But Jane's father felt that she should be educated and prepared for whatever she chose to do. So, Jane went to Rockford Seminary for Females (now Rockford College, Illinois) and received a degree in 1882. Her father's death that year and her own poor health sent her wandering around Europe with her college roommate, Ellen Gates Starr.

In the wretched slums of East London these young women of privilege visited the famous Toynbee Hall settlement house. It was there that Jane Addams found her career, although it was perhaps not quite what her father had imagined.

Addams and Starr were deeply moved by the miserable conditions of the poor in England and what Toynbee Hall was trying to do for those people. It gave them a sense of purpose. Perhaps they could use their wealth and education to ease the problems of the poor in their own country.

Back home, on September 18, 1889, Addams and Starr opened Hull House in the dirty, overcrowded industrial center of Chicago's Near West Side. The large vacant building, built by Chicago businessman Charles Hull, was more than thirty years old. It stood in the midst of a huge immigrant population that flocked to Chicago during the latter decades of the nineteenth century. Hull House would be home and workplace for Addams until her death in 1935. It would gain an international reputation through her work and that of Starr and other reformers who lived there. Jane Addams became one of the country's most prominent women and fighters for world peace.

But when Hull House opened, no one knew anything about this well-bred, well-educated twenty-nine-year-old woman. She was gentle, able, independent, and generous. She was also determined. She was determined to use Hull House as a way to bring culture, pride, and opportunity to the thousands of poor immigrants who lived in the area. They were mostly Catholic and Jewish, from Italy, Greece, and Russia and other eastern European countries. Few spoke English. Most were uneducated. Their clothes and culture seemed strange to many native-born Americans. And because they were different, they were often regarded and treated as inferior.

Jane Addams thought differently. She said that these new Americans were poor not because they were inferior but because they lacked the opportunity and know-how to better themselves. She and the other women of Hull House tried to change that. Over the next decades Hull House established many firsts: Chicago's first public playground and swimming pool, the first citizenship preparation classes and free art exhibits, the first Boy Scout troop, the first little theater in the United States, the first factory inspector in Illinois. Hull House investigations led to the first factory laws in the state and the first tenement code. Four labor unions, including the Women Shirt Makers, were organized at Hull House. A day nursery was set up for working mothers, as well as a community kitchen, an employment bureau, training in such crafts as bookbinding, and college-level courses.

Jane Addams was so intent on improving life for the people of the neighborhood that she got herself appointed garbage inspector. She rose at 6 A.M. to follow the neighborhood trash collectors to make sure that the job was done correctly.

For all these improvements, perhaps the greatest work by Jane Addams and Hull House was the laws they helped to pass. Illinois enacted a child labor law in 1903, limiting how long a child could work. This was followed by a law that said children must go to school until a certain age. Hull House helped to get the working day for women reduced to eight hours, as well as laws that aided workers who were hurt or got sick on the job. These efforts were greatly rewarded on the national level when the Federal Children's Bureau was created in 1912 and a federal child-labor law was passed in 1916.

The name of Jane Addams gained national recognition. Some called her the "greatest American who ever lived." In 1910 she became the first woman president of the National Conference of Social Work. She was on the boards of numerous organizations, such as the National Child Labor Committee. She vigorously supported the right of women to vote, becoming vice president of the National American Woman Suffrage Association.

Throughout her life she wrote eleven books and hundreds of articles, most of them dealing with the work of Hull House, with women's issues, and with peace. For Jane Addams these three issues were joined together. She strongly felt that there would be peace in the world when there was no more poverty and when people were allowed to grow. She believed that women could lead the way in this effort.

Jane Addams was greatly saddened by the outbreak of World War I in Europe in 1914. She began to speak out against the fighting on both sides, equating war deaths with murder. In 1915 she met with other women-for-peace at a vast conference in Washington, D.C. The Women's Peace Party was formed, with Addams as the chairperson. The party urged warring nations to talk instead of fight. It wanted to stop sending aid to countries that fired guns. Young people, declared the party, should be educated in the ways of peace.

Also in 1915, Addams attended the International Congress of Women at The Hague in the Netherlands. From 1919 to 1929 she was president of this organization, which became the Women's International League for Peace and Freedom. Its members, all women pacifists, were committed to the cause of world peace and freedom.

Despite protests World War I raged on. The United States officially entered the war against Germany in 1917. When President Woodrow Wilson urged all Americans, even those who opposed the fighting, to join in the war effort, Addams refused. She fervently believed that war was wrong and that fighting was an immoral act.

However, America at war was in no mood to tolerate a pacifist—even the popular Jane Addams. Hers now became a name to be booed and shunned. Newspapers called her unpatriotic and a Communist. The war ended in 1918. Addams urged a great international effort to end the mass starvation that spread throughout Europe after the war. For that, everyone cheered her name. Then she said that the Germans should be included as well. For that, she was branded a traitor.

No matter what they called her, Jane Addams stayed true to her beliefs. In 1920 she helped to found the American Civil Liberties Union, which still fights for citizens' rights under the Constitution. And, as always, there was the work of Hull House. Through the years, and with the dedicated help of many residents, Hull House added buildings as well as programs and summer camps. Some of Chicago's wealthiest men and women were often seen helping out. Prominent Chicagoan Jennie Dow founded and directed a kindergarten. Young Frances Perkins offered a helping hand. She later became the first woman to serve in a presidential cabinet, as Franklin D. Roosevelt's secretary of labor from 1933 to 1945.

Jane Addams (center)
and members of the
American delegation
arrive at The Hague,
in the Netherlands.

Evening mealtime at Hull House was likely to be an exciting affair. The residents never knew if they would be talking to poet Carl Sandburg, architect Frank Lloyd Wright, attorney Clarence Darrow, or perhaps J. Ramsey MacDonald, future prime minister of Great Britain. They all visited Hull House.

Some famous people also attended classes there. Benny Goodman, an immigrant tailor's son and the future King of Swing, took music lessons. Arthur Goldberg, whose father was a poor fruit and vegetable peddler, went there too. In later years President John F. Kennedy appointed Goldberg to the U.S. Supreme Court. Hyman Rickover, also the son of a tailor, studied at Hull House. Later, as Admiral Rickover, he would be called the "Father of the Nuclear Navy."

Through the years most of the furor about Jane Addams the pacifist or Jane Addams the traitor died down as she continued her work. Her efforts were finally recognized worldwide when she was given the Nobel Peace Prize in 1931. She shared the award with American educator Nicholas Murray Butler.

Four years later, in 1935, Jane Addams died in a Chicago hospital. Her partner and cofounder of Hull House, Ellen Gates Starr, died five years later. Addams is buried in her hometown of Cedarville—still a moon away from Hull House. On the day of her death most of the businesses in the Hull House area closed down in her honor.

In 1963 the University of Illinois needed the land around Hull House for its Chicago campus, so the Hull House organization moved to a new site. But the original building, at the corner of Polk and Halsted streets and now on the campus of the University of Illinois at Chicago, has been declared a National Historic Landmark as the Jane Addams' Hull House Museum. The interior has been restored to look as it did when Addams and Starr opened it. Visitors are invited daily for a tour through the building, a lasting memorial to the woman whom early immigrants to America called the "saint of Halsted Street."

WOODROW WILSON

(1856-1924)

TWENTY-EIGHTH PRESIDENT OF
THE UNITED STATES; WINNER,
1919 NOBEL PEACE PRIZE

**Wilson devoted most of his time and
energy after World War I to establishing a League of Nations dedicated to
world peace.**

Thomas Woodrow Wilson was a
Southerner, born in Staunton,
Virginia, on December 28,
1856. His mother, Janet ("Jessie"), had emigrated from England. His
father, Joseph, was a stern Presbyterian minister from Ohio. The third
of four children, Woodrow spent his early years in Georgia and South
Carolina. He never forgot the suffering he saw in the South during the
Civil War (1861–1865) and the years just after. All through his life, he
was firmly opposed to war.

The young boy's keen mind set him apart from friends his own
age. After a year at Davidson College in North Carolina, he entered
the College of New Jersey (now Princeton University) in 1875. Although he took part in debates and public speaking, Wilson did not
strive to earn high marks. He graduated in 1879 in the middle of his
class.

Having decided on a career in government, Wilson entered law
school at the University of Virginia. His poor health, however, took
him out of the classroom to a law practice in Atlanta, Georgia. But
Wilson the intellectual seemed ill suited to deal with everyday law

Woodrow Wilson's opposition to war became a guiding principle of his life.

problems. In 1883, with no clients in his office, he left Georgia for Johns Hopkins University in Baltimore, Maryland.

Three years later Wilson had a doctor's degree in government and a wife. He had married Ellen Louise Axson of Savannah, Georgia, on June 24, 1885. The young couple went to Bryn Mawr College in Pennsylvania, where Wilson taught history and political economy. This happy marriage produced three daughters.

Wilson's career now began a rapid rise. After Bryn Mawr he taught at Wesleyan University in Connecticut until 1890, when Princeton University asked him to join the faculty. He was not yet thirty-four years old, only eleven years out of college himself. In 1902 he was named president of Princeton.

Wilson now began to attract statewide attention because of his articles and speeches on government and politics of the day. Then, leading New Jersey Democrats discovered him. Here was an ideal candidate. He was honest, intelligent, and articulate. He believed in the rights of the people, even though many claimed he was biased against black Americans and other minorities.

The Democrats were right about Wilson as a candidate. In 1910 he was elected governor of New Jersey.

Within a few months, national leaders began to take notice of the new governor. He fought for laws against corrupt practices in state government and for making employers responsible for their actions against their workers.

In June 1912 the Democratic convention chose Woodrow Wilson as its presidential candidate. This was the Democrats' lucky year. The Republican party was split in two because of a personal quarrel between Theodore Roosevelt and William Howard Taft. Wilson was elected the twenty-eighth president of the United States with 435 electoral votes against 88 for Roosevelt and 8 for Taft.

After the death of his first wife, Wilson married Edith Bolling Galt in 1915. He was remarkably active during his first term, pushing for many government reforms. His foreign policy was marked by respect for the rights and interests of small countries. But soon Wilson and the United States faced a real war with Mexico, which had just gone through a civil war of its own. The loser, Pancho Villa, attacked a town in New Mexico, hoping the United States would attack Mexico in return and start a war. Many Americans did urge Wilson to fight, but the peace-loving president instead decided to "watch and wait." Although the Mexican revolution was a worry to Wilson throughout his administration, there was no war.

Wilson successfully used the slogan "He kept us out of war" for his reelection campaign of 1916. But a greater problem than Mexico was World War I, which had started in Europe two years earlier. True to his peace policy, Wilson tried desperately to keep the United States from becoming involved. Eventually, however, government pressures at home and abroad, public opinion, and German attacks on U.S. ships were too strong. The president reluctantly asked Congress for a declaration of war on April 6, 1917.

Although Wilson hated war, once he had committed the nation to it he proved to be a forceful, intelligent commander. He gave Americans the feeling that World War I was a just conflict in which all citizens must make sacrifices. And he let the leaders in key military and government positions do their jobs with a minimum of interference.

In January 1918 Wilson gave his famous Fourteen Points speech to the U.S. Congress. In it he outlined factors he believed would create a just and lasting world peace, such as open talks among nations, freedom of the seas, and reduction of arms. World War I ended with victory for the United States and its allies on November 11, 1918. In January, Wilson attended the Paris Peace Conference. He insisted that a League of Nations must be part of the peace treaty. He said, "To conquer with arms is only temporary. To conquer the world by earning its esteem is permanent. We must establish peace among the nations." He believed that a League of Nations, where problems would be discussed openly, would prevent fighting.

The conference members finally agreed to include the League in the Versailles peace treaty. In the main, Wilson's work was done. All that was left was approval of the treaty by the U.S. Senate. But some senators wanted changes before they would sign. Wilson refused any changes whatsoever. He had always taken a very high-handed, moral approach to what he believed in. Now he became stubborn.

Wilson spent much of 1919 touring the country trying to convince Americans of the need for the League of Nations.

The more the opposition demanded, the more stubborn the President became. He spent much of 1919 touring the country, crusading for his cause. The stress began to show on his fragile health. In October he suffered a stroke that partially paralyzed his left side. During the worst of his illness his wife kept most government business from him, and it was said that she assumed much of the responsibility of the president's office.

Perhaps had Wilson recovered fully, he would have seen the value of compromise. In his weakened condition he did not. He stuck to his position. If there were changes to the treaty, he would not sign it. Ironically, the one person above all who worked for the League of Nations caused it to fail. The Senate did not ratify the treaty. The League lasted until 1946, but its influence, especially without the United States, was minimal, and World War II proved its uselessness. It did, however, pave the way for the establishment of the United Nations in 1945.

Partially recovered, Wilson was awarded the 1919 Nobel Peace Prize in December 1920. That may have eased the blow of the next presidential election, which brought in Republican Warren G. Harding in 1921. Still heartbroken over the failure of the League of Nations, Wilson made no reference to it in his last message to Congress.

Woodrow Wilson lived quietly in Washington, D.C., until his death on February 3, 1924. An intelligent leader with a rigid sense of responsibility, he used his office to "wield the sword of speech." Although his refusal to compromise might sometimes have cost him victory, he is above all remembered as a man who believed in and worked tirelessly for peace.

MOHANDAS GANDHI

(1869-1948)

INDIAN NATIONALIST AND
SPIRITUAL LEADER

With his decision to gain India's freedom by peacefully defying authority, Gandhi became the prophet of nonviolence in the twentieth century.

Mohandas Karamchand Gandhi might seem an unlikely figure to have led India's fight for independence. He was a small, frail-looking youth who grew into a small, frail-looking adult. He was a so-so student, "good in English and weak in geography." He was poor in sports and liked to take long walks by himself. And, according to the traditions of his family's religion, he was married at the age of thirteen to a girl he did not know.

Yet from this background came one of history's strongest and most dedicated fighters for freedom by peaceful means.

Gandhi was the youngest of four children, born on October 2, 1869, in Porbandar, Gujarat, India, then under British rule. His father, Karamchand, was the region's chief minister, as his grandfather had been. His mother, Putlibai, was deeply religious. She worshiped the Hindu god Vishnu, who taught nonviolence, fasting, tolerance, and vegetarianism. Gandhi later admitted that as a teenager he rebelled by eating meat.

In 1881 Gandhi was married to Kasturbai Makanji, another thirteen-year-old from Porbandar. Her father was a well-to-do mer-

A frail figure in simple, peasant clothes, Mohandas Gandhi developed methods of peaceful protest that spread far beyond his native India.

chant, but Kasturbai could not read or write. Her new husband taught her. Although the young couple had not known each other before the marriage, their union would be lasting. The Gandhis would have four sons, Harilal, Manilal, Ramdas, and Devadas.

Although he was married at thirteen, Gandhi was not free to decide his own future. He preferred the field of medicine, but his family chose the law so that he could carry on the Gandhi tradition of government work. Education for the law meant school in England. Over his mother's objections—she was afraid he would break Hindu vows in a foreign land—Gandhi sailed for England in 1888 without his young wife.

The three years at a law college in London were not easy for this pitifully shy lad. But as he struggled with his studies and the ridicule of his friends for not eating meat, Gandhi began to take on an unaccustomed poise. When he returned to India in 1891, he was ready to begin a new life.

However, Gandhi soon discovered that a new life was not going to be easy. Both his parents were now dead, he had his own family to care for, and there were already too many lawyers in India. So, in 1893 he accepted a job for one year with an Indian firm in Natal, South Africa. There Gandhi first experienced the way in which white South Africans treated people "of color," a term that included Indians as well as blacks. He was barred from hotels for "Europeans only," beaten by white bigots, and thrown out of first-class railway cars. These experiences changed the normally docile Gandhi into a man determined to defend his own dignity.

His year's contract ended, Gandhi prepared to leave for home. On the eve of departure, he heard that the South African government was considering a law to take voting rights away from Indians. His Indian friends begged him to stay and fight for their cause. Gandhi agreed.

For all of his life, this shy and frail young man had been terrified of making a speech or even talking at a social gathering. Until he was eighteen he had hardly ever read a newspaper and had never shown any interest in politics. Now, at the age of twenty-five, he became a dedicated political campaigner.

For the next seven years, Gandhi fought through peaceful means for Indian rights in South Africa. He organized the Natal Indian Congress. He petitioned the government. He spoke at public meetings. He gained attention in the press for exposing the plight of Indians and other minorities. When the Boer War erupted in 1899, pitting the Boers (Dutch settlers) against Great Britain's rule, Gandhi declared that if Indians wanted citizenship rights, they must defend the government, and he organized an ambulance corps of volunteers.

For all his efforts, Gandhi was nearly lynched by a white mob, and the British victory in the Boer War brought little relief to the Indian minority. But Gandhi, even if he did not yet realize it, had found what would be his lifelong method of battle: fighting without violence.

In 1915 Gandhi returned to his homeland, still under British control. Although he wanted a free India, he seemed uncertain of what to do about it. He would not join a political party but quietly participated in movements for independence. He supported the British during World War I, even recruiting soldiers for the British Indian Army. He did not call for any physical action for independence, but he was not afraid to criticize British rule in public. As he did so, his reputation grew.

Then, in 1919, Britain pushed through the Rowlatt Bills. The aim was to stamp out opposition to British rule in India by allowing imprisonment without trial. Gandhi spoke out, telling his countrymen to oppose this law. The result was a shock, both to the British and to Gandhi. The British were shocked because of the violence that erupted in many Indian cities. Nearly four hundred Indians were killed in a riot in the city of Amritsar. Gandhi was shocked because he had not realized he had become such a popular figure. And he was saddened by the violence because he had urged Indians to oppose the new law peacefully.

By the end of 1919 Gandhi had become the major figure in Indian politics. As such, he stated that the people of India should counter British rule peacefully. This method of battle, which he had begun in South Africa, was now in full bloom under the name of nonviolent noncooperation. It would make the name of Mohandas Gandhi world famous.

It is unlikely that Gandhi could have devoted himself so tirelessly and so successfully to his nonviolent cause without the cooperation of his wife, Kasturbai. From an uneducated, simple woman, she became a tower of strength to Gandhi, raising their family and devoting herself wholeheartedly to his work. She was imprisoned for leading the fight for women's rights in India. She became the leader of the independence movement whenever her famous husband was imprisoned. Deeply religious, she denounced all forms of bigotry and stood firmly in her beliefs until her death in 1944.

From 1920 until Gandhi's own death in 1948, he would be imprisoned many times as he struggled for Indian freedom from the British. He fashioned the Indian National Congress party into an effective political force. In 1922 he was arrested for civil disobedience—nonviolent protest—and was sent to jail for six years. He was released in 1924 after an appendicitis operation.

Upon his release Gandhi was elected president of the Indian National Congress. In 1930 he led a nonviolent fight against the unfair Salt Tax, which most affected the poor. This was one of his most successful campaigns, resulting in 60,000 arrests as Indians openly, but peacefully, defied the government. Once more Gandhi was imprisoned, but his peaceful methods had caught fire with the Indian people. Realizing this, the British decided to try cooperation. They released Gandhi and invited him to attend a conference in London as the only representative of the Indian National Congress. But Gandhi was bitterly disappointed to discover that the conference concerned only the problems of Indian minorities, not the transfer of government power from the British to the Indian people.

Gandhi renewed his campaign of nonviolent disobedience and was back in prison in 1932. The British government announced its intention to set up a separate voting body for India's lowest economic class, known as the Untouchables. These people were treated as outcasts in Indian society. Gandhi opposed this voting division and declared that he would fast until his death to prevent it. He also renamed the Untouchables, calling them Harijans, "Children of God."

A compromise was reached that ended Gandhi's fast, but when he declared another fast for the Harijans in 1933, the British promptly released him from jail. In 1934 Gandhi resigned from the Indian National Congress to devote his time to the Harijan cause and Indian freedom.

When the British entered World War II, Gandhi was back in politics once again. Although he was against using the war to gain an upper hand against Britain, he was dismayed when India was thrown into the conflict without its consent. In 1942 he urged the Congress party to adopt the "Quit India" resolution. It demanded that the British leave the country immediately. For that, Gandhi, his wife, and party leaders were all thrown in jail, where Kasturbai died. Gandhi was released in 1944.

By now the British sensed that the battle to retain India was lost. In 1946 an assembly met to decide the fate of the country. But there were so many fights and disagreements among Hindus and Muslims and other factions that riots broke out and spread across the country. So, when British rule was ended on August 15, 1947, the result was not one new nation, but two—India and Pakistan.

It was one of the great disappointments of Gandhi's life that all his years of struggle for Indian freedom resulted in bitter hatred between Hindu and Muslim and a breakup of his beloved land. As riots between the two groups continued after the partition, Gandhi tried to bring peace. In that atmosphere at that time, it was an impossible task even for him. When persuasion failed, Gandhi went on a hunger strike. In this he was successful. His fasting stopped a riot in Calcutta in September 1947 and brought a truce to the city of Delhi in January 1948.

The hatred between Hindu and Muslim, however, did not end. On January 30, 1948, on the way to a prayer meeting in Delhi, Mohandas Gandhi was shot to death by a young Hindu fanatic. The violence did not end even there. Some 200,000 people died in rioting as Muslim refugees fled to Pakistan and Hindu refugees to India in a mass crossover of people. Violent clashes have continued through the years, just as Gandhi feared when he heard of the partition decision. In the 1990s, clashes continue to break out between these two groups, and relations between India and Pakistan remain strained.

With Gandhi's death in 1948, India, and the world, lost a great fighter for peace, a man of ideas and of action, a man of religion, and a political leader as well. The British regarded him with amusement at first, then suspicion and resentment. Within his own country he was criticized for going too fast, or not fast enough. Muslims declared him partial to the Hindu cause. Even the leaders of the Harijans, Gandhi's Children of God, doubted his worth as a social reformer. But if Gandhi's political role in India was exaggerated through the years, the success of his peaceful protests was not. Except for a few leaders, such as Martin Luther King, Jr., in the United States, not many have been able to follow his methods and ideals. He truly believed that nonviolence is the way to guarantee freedom of religion and democracy. To millions of his countrymen, he is Mahatma, "the great soul."

Ralph Bunche's work with the United Nations brought him a Nobel Peace Prize.

RALPH BUNCHE
(1904-1971)

UNDERSECRETARY-GENERAL OF
THE UNITED NATIONS; WINNER,
1950 NOBEL PEACE PRIZE

**The Nobel Peace Prize honored Bunche
for his tireless efforts to bring peace
to the Middle East through the
United Nations.**

Ralph J. Bunche was a black American who, as he once said in a speech at the United Nations, lived through a period that was "just about the most turbulent in history." He was speaking of the twenty-five years from 1945 to 1970. This was a time of wars abroad—World War II, Korea, Vietnam—and wars at home: increasing bitterness over segregation, protest marches and riots, and the fight for civil rights legislation. Through all this, quietly but firmly, walked a man of peace.

Ralph Bunche was born in Detroit, Michigan, on August 7, 1904. His father, Fred, was a barber, his mother, Olive Agnes, a homemaker. The Bunches had one other child, named Grace.

By the time Ralph was thirteen, both his parents had died, and he and Grace were cared for by their maternal grandmother, Lucy Johnson. Young Ralph went to schools in Detroit and in Albuquerque, New Mexico, graduating from high school in Los Angeles. From there he went on to earn a master's (1928) and a doctoral degree (1934) in government at Harvard University. He continued his schooling at Northwestern University (1936), the London School of Economics (1937), and South Africa's University of Cape Town

(1937). During this period he joined the faculty of Howard University in Washington, D.C., establishing a department of political science. He helped with the research on *An American Dilemma*, a monumental study of blacks in America published in 1944 by the Swedish sociologist Gunnar Myrdal.

Bunche married Ruth Ethel Harris of Montgomery, Alabama, a former schoolteacher and Howard University graduate. They had three children, two daughters and a son.

Before World War II, Bunche spent a good deal of time in Africa studying colonial policies. When the United States entered the war, the State Department sought him out for his knowledge of African affairs. As the war raged on, representatives of four governments—China, Great Britain, the Soviet Union, and the United States—met at Dumbarton Oaks, a mansion in Washington, D.C., in 1944 to lay the groundwork for what later became the United Nations. Bunche was named a member of the U.S. delegation. He was also active at the 1945 San Francisco conference that set up the United Nations.

The UN was officially born on October 24, 1945, when representatives of all the participating countries signed its charter. The first UN General Assembly met in London in 1946 and decided that permanent UN headquarters should be built in the United States. New York City was chosen.

With John D. Rockefeller, Jr.'s, gift of $8.5 million to buy land along the East River in New York City, and more land donated by the city itself, four UN buildings soon became part of New York's famous skyline: the General Assembly building, the Secretariat tower, the Conference building, and the Dag Hammarskjöld Library.

From its headquarters the work of the UN is carried out in all parts of the world through six main bodies.

The *General Assembly* is the main division. All UN members are represented, each nation has one vote, and all can be heard on any matter. The General Assembly meets for about three months each year and appoints the secretary-general, who runs the UN.

The fifteen-member *Security Council* is the UN's guardian of peace. The five permanent members—China, France, Great Britain, the Russian Federation (formerly the Soviet Union), and the United States—are joined by ten members whom the General Assembly elects for two-year terms. The Security Council does not meet regularly and deals only with questions of peace and security. A "no" vote from any of the five permanent members kills any resolution.

The *Economic and Social Council (ECOSOC)* has fifty-four member countries, which the General Assembly elects for three-year terms. It usually meets twice a year on any questions concerned with economics, such as trade or industrialization.

The five permanent members of the Security Council make up the *Trusteeship Council*, and they usually meet once a year. Originally in charge of eleven Trust Territories—parts of the world where the people could not choose their own governments—the Council today supervises only one such territory, the Pacific Islands, which is administered by the United States.

The *International Court of Justice* is in permanent session at The Hague, the Netherlands. Only countries, not people, can present cases before the Court. The fifteen judges are elected by the General Assembly, and no two can come from the same country.

The *Secretariat*, with a staff of about 25,000 people worldwide, carries out the day-to-day work of the UN. It is headed by the secretary-general, who is the chief UN officer and appointed for a term of five years. The UN has had only six secretaries-general since it began: Norway's Trygve Lie (appointed in 1946); Sweden's Dag Hammarskjöld (1953), discussed in the next chapter; Burma's U Thant (1961); Austria's Kurt Waldheim (1972); Peru's Javier Pérez de Cuéllar (1982); and Egypt's Boutros Boutros-Ghali (1992).

In 1947, at the request of the UN, Ralph Bunche resigned from the U.S. State Department to accept a permanent position with the Secretariat. Before the birth of the state of Israel, Secretary-General Trygve Lie asked him to help settle a dispute in Palestine between Arabs and Jews. Bunche found himself in the spotlight when the UN's chief mediator in Palestine, Count Folke Bernadotte, was assassinated in 1948. As acting UN mediator, Bunche got the warring sides to agree to an armistice the following year. For that effort he won the Nobel Peace Prize in 1950.

Bunche's peacekeeping abilities earned him a promotion to UN Undersecretary for Special Political Affairs. He worked directly for the UN's second secretary-general, Dag Hammarskjöld, as a troubleshooter. In 1956 there was plenty of trouble in the Middle East. On July 26 Egypt's president, Gamal Abdel Nasser, took over the Suez Canal, the vital waterway that connects the Mediterranean and Red seas and separates Africa from Asia. Nasser was angry because the United States and Great Britain would not give money to help build the Aswan High Dam on the Nile River. (It was finally finished with Soviet aid.) In protest against Nasser's actions, Israel sent troops to the area. Britain and France did the same. To avert what seemed a likely war, the UN told Israel, Britain, and France to get out and sent in six thousand UN troops to keep the peace. Bunche was sent over to supervise the UN force. There was no war—that time. In 1960 and 1964 the UN sent Ralph Bunche on similar peacekeeping missions to the Congo and then Cyprus.

Now a well-known international figure, Bunche began to hear criticism of himself at home from black Americans for neglecting the civil rights movement. And, indeed, despite his frequent travels and high position, Bunche had experienced the pain of prejudice. Even after he had won the Nobel Peace Prize, for instance, in Washington, D.C., the nation's capital, he ordered theater tickets speaking French. In this way the ticket sellers would not think he was a black American and therefore refuse him tickets.

Stung by the criticism, Bunche began to speak out against injustice and prejudice in the United States. Although in poor health, he took part in the 1965 civil rights marches in Selma and Montgomery, Alabama, and served on the board of the National Association for the Advancement of Colored People (NAACP). The NAACP, founded in 1909, is an interracial organization that works against racism and for the civil rights of black Americans and other minorities.

When Bunche was sent on a mission for the UN, his task was always the same—to avert war if possible. He was remarkably good at it. Bunche had the ability to listen to different sides, to make people listen to him, to remain calm and reasonable in a crisis, and to offer worthwhile alternatives. That was his great contribution to world peace.

Ralph Johnson Bunche died in New York City on December 9, 1971. He was perhaps without equal as a peace mediator.

Bunche greets Egyptian president Nasser on a 1957 peace mission to the Middle East.

As UN secretary-general, Dag Hammarskjöld traveled all over the world, using personal diplomacy to help make the United Nations a force for world peace.

DAG HAMMARSKJÖLD

(1905-1961)

SECRETARY-GENERAL OF THE
UNITED NATIONS; WINNER,
1961 NOBEL PEACE PRIZE

**Dag Hammarskjöld gave his life trying
to prove that the United Nations could
be a peacemaking, not just a peacekeeping, world force.**

On September 18, 1961, a helicopter carrying Dag Hjalmar Agne Carl Hammarskjöld on a peace mission went down in the African jungle, and the UN secretary-general was killed.

A tropical forest in Africa was a long way from the university town of Uppsala, Sweden, where Hammarskjöld grew up. Born in Jönköping in south-central Sweden on July 29, 1905, Dag was the fourth son of Knut Hjalmar and Agnes Hammarskjöld. His father became Sweden's prime minister during World War I and later was chairman of the Nobel Prize Foundation.

Young Hammarskjöld studied law and economics at Uppsala until he moved to Stockholm in 1930. There he became secretary of a government committee on unemployment and attended the University of Stockholm. He received a doctorate in economics in 1933 and took a teaching job on the university faculty.

At the age of thirty-one, Hammarskjöld joined the Swedish civil service in the Ministry of Finance. For the next few years he served as chairman of the board of the National Bank of Sweden. During and after World War II he helped to shape Sweden's money policies and advised his government on many economic problems.

By 1947, Hammarskjöld had joined the Swedish Foreign Office, where, as undersecretary, he was responsible for all financial questions. He was a delegate to the Paris Conference, which set up the European Recovery Program, better known as the Marshall Plan. It was named for the man who proposed it, U.S. general George C. Marshall, World War II hero and later secretary of state and secretary of defense.

Hammarskjöld was the chairman of the Swedish delegation to the United Nations in 1953 when Marshall was awarded the Nobel Peace Prize for his work in rebuilding a war-torn Europe. Also in that year, on April 10, Hammarskjöld was elected secretary-general of the United Nations. Five months earlier, Trygve Lie of Norway, the UN's first secretary-general, had resigned. He did so largely because of trouble with the Soviet Union. The Soviets were angered in 1950 because Lie authorized the use of UN troops to aid South Korea in its fight against North Korea. The Russians backed the Communist North Koreans.

Hammarskjöld was elected to a five-year term as the UN's leader, and in 1957 to a second term. The secretary-general of the United Nations functions much like the president of any large corporation or country. It is his job—so far only men have held the post—to see that everything in the UN runs smoothly. He acts as referee when member countries disagree. He brings problems that threaten world peace to the attention of the Security Council. He proposes issues that should be discussed in the General Assembly or any of the other UN divisions.

During Hammarskjöld's first years as the UN's chief officer, the world was relatively free of international troubles. He used the time to build public confidence in his office and in the United Nations as an organization. He had high regard for the UN as a peace force and was greatly concerned that it would become too dominated by the United States, its biggest financial contributor. He also insisted that as secretary-general he must be able to take action in an emergency without the prior approval of the General Assembly or Security Council. A quiet but strongly determined leader, Hammarskjöld gained much respect inside the UN and throughout the world for his moral force and steady diplomacy.

After the first years Hammarskjöld stepped into high gear. In 1954 he visited Peking, China. Soon after, the Chinese People's Republic released fifteen American fliers who had been held since the Korean War (1950–1953). He traveled throughout the Americas, Asia, and Africa getting to know the heads of governments and the problems of the areas.

Increasingly, Hammarskjöld became worried about the troubled Middle East. The Arab states and Israel were always either fighting or threatening to fight. The secretary-general used his position and influence to calm a dispute between Lebanon and Jordan. In 1956, along with Canadian statesman Lester Pearson, he helped to stop a possible war in the Middle East when trouble erupted after Egypt's president, Gamal Abdel Nasser, took over the Suez Canal. Under Hammarskjöld's leadership the UN sent a peacekeeping force and mediator Ralph Bunche to avert war. It worked.

As the 1960s began, however, Hammarskjöld's attention was directed toward troubles in Africa. In 1960 the small nation of the Belgian Congo was granted independence; it later became the country known as Zaire. After independence the nation suffered severe growing pains. The United Nations was called in to avert an all-out civil war. Eventually, the UN forces were able to restore order and stop the shooting.

Hammarskjöld made several trips to the area in an effort to bring peace. On his fourth journey, 6 miles (10 kilometers) from the Ndola airport in Northern Rhodesia (now Zambia), that fatal helicopter crash occurred in the jungle.

Shocked and saddened people everywhere mourned the death of this tireless worker for the cause of peace throughout the world. In 1961, shortly after his death, he was awarded the Nobel Peace Prize.

Dag Hammarskjöld was a man who profoundly believed in the United Nations. As he said of his role as secretary-general in a speech following his unanimous election to a second term: "If it paves one more inch of the road ahead, one is more than rewarded by what is achieved . . . every step forward in the pioneer effort of this organization inevitably widens the scope for the fight for peace."

*At a cabinet meeting
in 1977, Jimmy Carter
shows the unpretentious
image that was a mark
of his presidency.*

JIMMY CARTER
(1924-   )

THIRTY-NINTH PRESIDENT
OF THE UNITED STATES

"Are we going to sit here until the end
of our lives and see another generation come along with an increasing
number of wars going on every year?"
Jimmy Carter, speech to the
International Negotiation Network,
January 15, 1992

James Earl Carter, Jr., or Jimmy Carter, as he is known around the world, was the first U.S. president in well over a century to come from the South. Woodrow Wilson was born a Southerner, but he campaigned for the presidency in 1912 as the governor of the northeastern state of New Jersey. Carter, a Georgia peanut farmer and one-term governor of Georgia, won national and world respect both during and after his four years in office for his devotion to the cause of peace. He also put the town of Plains, Georgia—population 550—on the map.

James Earl Jr. was born in Plains on October 1, 1924. His father, James Earl Sr., was called Earl, and his mother, Lillian Gordy Carter, was better known as Miss Lillian. Jimmy, his two sisters, Gloria and Ruth, and his brother, Billy, grew up in and around Plains. Young Jimmy's father was strict. He believed his boys should work for a living. From the time he was six, Jimmy had to get up for farm chores along with everyone else.

(47)

In high school Jimmy was a brilliant student and a mediocre basketball player. He was also shy and short, 5 feet 3 inches (160 centimeters); he eventually stretched another 7 inches (18 centimeters).

After high school, Carter went to Georgia Southwestern College for a year and then to the Georgia Institute of Technology in Atlanta to study math. He was working toward his dream, an appointment to the U.S. Naval Academy at Annapolis, Maryland. Carter entered the Academy in 1943 in the middle of World War II and graduated in 1946 as an ensign. On July 7 of that year he married Rosalyn Smith, whom he had known since childhood. The Carters have three sons, John William, James Earl III, and Jeffrey, and one daughter, Amy.

For the next seven years Carter served on battleships and submarines. He resigned from the Navy in 1953 with the rank of lieutenant commander. His father's death took him back home to Georgia to manage the family business. Part of the business included peanut farming, at which Carter became very successful.

Businessman Carter took an interest in civic affairs over the next few years and ran for the state senate in 1962. He lost. But he believed the election results were phony, so he challenged them in court. He won the court challenge and therefore the election, and he was later elected to a second term. His voting record was moderate. In 1965, when the Plains Baptist Church was deciding whether to bar blacks from the congregation, Carter gave an impassioned speech asking them not to. That earned him some enemies among southern whites, but it also earned him a reputation as a liberal on race relations.

Still largely unknown in his state, Carter sought the Democratic nomination for governor of Georgia in 1966. Staunch segregationist Lester G. Maddox won both the ticket and the election. After Carter's defeat, he became a "born-again" Christian and tried for the governorship once more in 1970. This time he campaigned up and down the state, getting known and declaring himself just a "simple country boy." It worked. Carter won the Democratic nomination and then the governorship.

Because he had run a conservative campaign to get himself elected, there was much doubt about his "liberal" attitude. In fact, the Atlanta *Constitution* had called him "an ignorant, racist, red-necked South Georgia peanut farmer." But Governor Carter soon cleared up all doubts on the issue. In his inaugural speech on January 12, 1971, he told his fellow Georgians, "I say to you quite frankly that the time for racial discrimination is over." Carter was touted as a governor of the "New South."

In 1974, just before his term ended, the governor announced that he would enter the presidential race in 1976. He was still little known outside his own state, although he was regarded as an effective governor in Georgia. With tireless persistence and following a precise strategy mapped out by his friend Hamilton Jordan, who would later become his chief Washington aide, Carter broadened his knowledge of foreign affairs and crisscrossed the country. He told anyone who would listen that he "was just one of the regular people" and proceeded to act that way. When he won the Democratic nomination for president, he chose liberal U.S. senator Walter Mondale of Minnesota as his running mate. The Democratic ticket, with just a little over 51 percent of the vote, won a narrow victory over the Republican incumbent, Gerald Ford. Jimmy Carter became the thirty-ninth president of the United States on January 20, 1977.

Carter ran his administration as he had run his campaign, as one of the people. He cut out the limousine service for his staff; he turned down the thermostat in the White House to save on fuel; his clothes were often casual and his style easy at meetings and on television; his first official act was to pardon the draft resisters from the Vietnam War.

Increasing involvement in Vietnam from 1956 to 1975 had nearly torn the United States apart. Many people had been bitterly opposed to U.S. troops being sent there. Some young men had been so against serving there that they had fled to Canada or elsewhere to escape the military draft. When Carter pardoned them and said they could return home, not all Americans were happy. Those who had fought in Vietnam felt betrayed by the President. The families of many veterans, especially of those killed or wounded, felt that men who had refused to defend their country should not be allowed to return without punishment. But Jimmy Carter, the man of peace, saw nothing to be gained by what struck him as revenge. The war was over. This should be a time of healing.

Carter tried to express his feelings of peace and healing to the country throughout his four years in office. He mentioned *peace* and *forgiveness* frequently in his speeches to the nation. He backed bills that focused on human and civil rights. He urged the country to forgive and live in harmony. He tried without much success to steer U.S. foreign policy toward greater concern with the civil rights of people in all nations.

No doubt, Jimmy Carter's greatest achievement for peace while in office was the Camp David Accords. In September 1978 he brought together the leaders of two countries that had been such long and bitter enemies that most people thought it would take a miracle just to get them to talk to each other, let alone sign a treaty. They were Anwar el-Sadat, president of Egypt, and Menachem Begin, prime minister of Israel. It looked like the miracle was Jimmy Carter. After two weeks at Camp David, a smiling U.S. president announced that terms for a peace treaty had been established between the two countries. The treaty was signed in Washington, D.C., on March 26, 1979.

If Camp David was President Carter's high point in office, the election of 1980 was the low. For this man of the people failed to inspire the confidence needed to be elected for a second term. After four years in office, Carter lost decisively to former actor and California governor Ronald Reagan. The Republicans even gained control of the Senate for the first time since 1954.

Why did this intelligent, likable man of the people lose? Historians say he lost for perhaps three reasons. Carter was never able to build a good working relationship with Congress, even though it was controlled by his own party. That gave the public the impression that he was an indecisive leader. He often got so tied up in the small details of an issue that he seemed to lose sight of the main points. That also sometimes made him appear uncertain. Even more damaging was his inability to free the American hostages seized by militants in Teheran, Iran, in November 1979. A U.S. military attempt to rescue

Carter shakes hands
with Anwar el-Sadat
of Egypt (left) and
Menachem Begin
of Israel (right) to
mark the signing of
the Camp David
Accords.

the hostages in April 1980 failed. They were not released until Reagan took office.

Jimmy Carter did emerge from his defeat, however, as a world leader for peace. After he left office, the ex-president seemed to be everywhere: helping to clean up a slum area in Atlanta, expertly using hammer and nails to help restore a depressed area in the Bronx, New York, visiting the desperately poor in Africa. In 1986 one of the great achievements of his postpresidential years was dedicated. It is the Carter Center in Atlanta, Georgia. This complex of nonprofit organizations seeks to ease conflicts, reduce suffering, and promote better understanding among all peoples. It also boasts of being the only institution in the world that keeps a former U.S. president involved in its activities on a day-to-day basis.

Members of the Carter Center become actively involved in peace issues throughout the United States and the world. In 1991, for instance, a group from the Center, led by Carter himself, went to Zambia in Africa to watch the first democratic election in the country's history. They wanted to make sure that the election was a fair one. The Center actively campaigns for such health issues as opposing cigarette smoking in developing countries or for a health-care program in some South American nations. Through publications and programs, television and other media campaigns, the Carter Center spreads the word about political, economic, and health-related issues that its members feel will help to ensure peace in the world.

Besides *the Office of Jimmy Carter*, the Carter Center has five other facilities:

1. *The Carter Center of Emory University (CCEU)*, which deals with public policy problems in the areas of Latin American and Caribbean studies, Middle Eastern studies, U.S.-Russian relations, African studies, international and domestic health issues, human rights, and conflict resolution.

2. *Global 2000 Inc.*, dedicated to improving health and agricultural services in developing countries.

(52)

3. *The Task Force for Child Survival (TFCS)*, which fosters immunization and other health benefits for children in developing countries.

4. *The Carter-Menil Human Rights Foundation*, which promotes the protection of human rights throughout the world.

5. *The Jimmy Carter Library and Museum*, which houses more than 27 million documents and is used as a research facility. It is operated by the National Archives.

Even more than when he was a world and political leader, Jimmy Carter, in his years since the White House, has become known as a world leader for peace. He is a smiling, soft-spoken, determined fighter among those who dedicate their lives to the idea that men and women can find a way to live side by side and country by country without bloodshed. As the former president says:

> War is a bestial thing. It is an inhuman thing—it violates basic human values, it ignores laws designed over the centuries that protect the right of one person living adjacent to another. . . . What can we do to make sure that this decade and the next decade will see a steady decrease in the incidence of war?

For Jimmy Carter, former peanut farmer, former governor, former president, the answer is to keep on working for the cause of peace, anywhere in the world that it takes him.

Desmond Tutu led nonviolent efforts to end apartheid, the South African system of racial segregation.

DESMOND TUTU
(1931-)

SOUTH AFRICAN ANGLICAN
BISHOP; WINNER,
1984 NOBEL PEACE PRIZE

Bishop Tutu was awarded the Nobel Peace Prize as "a renewed recognition of the courage and heroism shown by black South Africans in their use of peaceful methods in the struggle against apartheid."

Desmond Mpilo Tutu has called apartheid, the policy of racial discrimination that for so long ruled his native land, "as evil as Nazism." The Republic of South Africa, on the southernmost tip of the African continent, covers about 470,000 square miles (1.2 million square kilometers), or twice the size of Texas. Under apartheid some 4.5 million white South Africans held nearly total control over the lives of more than 23 million black South Africans. Only in the last two decades has a glimmer of hope and change started in this crippling system of separation and discrimination. Any true hope for future peace rests in the hands of Bishop Tutu and a few other leaders, both black and white, in South Africa.

How did this small nation on a continent dominated by blacks come to hold such a rigid policy of racial separation?

By the early 1700s both the English and the Dutch had established a lively trade with Asia. Their long and dangerous sailing route took them around the stormy Cape of Good Hope at the tip of Africa. They often stopped along the southwestern coast for fresh water and to trade with the natives for fresh meat. In 1652 the Dutch started a colony at what is now Cape Town, South Africa. The settlement thrived, although slowly. By the end of the century the settlers, of Dutch and German descent, numbered about 15,000. Calling themselves Afrikaners, they regarded South Africa as their only home. Some of them were known as Boers, seminomadic, rugged farmers who lived mainly outside of Cape Town.

In 1806 Britain seized the Cape colony, and many of the Boers trekked to the north where they founded two colonies of their own, the Transvaal and the Orange Free State. By the end of the 1800s the whole economy of the region was transformed with the discovery of enormous quantities of gold and diamonds.

Trouble between the British and the Boers broke out in 1899 with the South African, or Boer, War, which the British won in 1902. They created the Union of South Africa in 1910, joining the British Cape and Natal colonies with the Transvaal and the Orange Free State. The country became the Republic of South Africa in 1961 and withdrew from the British Commonwealth.

The government of South Africa had always practiced racial separation, or apartheid. This system grew out of the fierce desire of the white settlers to keep the larger native population "in their place." But in 1948, when the Nationalist party came to power, apartheid became the law. Its aims were to maintain white supremacy and to segregate the races as totally as possible.

Nonwhites outnumbered whites in South Africa by six to one. Nonwhites did not have the same rights as whites in voting, jobs, education, transportation, living quarters—or any other aspect of life. This was the culture into which a black South African, Desmond Mpilo Tutu, was born on October 7, 1931. His family lived in the gold-mining town of Klerksdorp in the Transvaal. Tutu's middle name means "life" in the Bantu language of Sotho. It was given to him by his grandmother because she did not expect the sickly baby to live.

But Desmond did live. His father, Zachariah, was a Methodist schoolteacher; his mother, Aletta, a domestic servant. The boy was educated in mission schools where his father taught. A gentle lad, he earned money by caddying at a golf course in Johannesburg, South Africa's largest city, and by selling peanuts at railroad stations. His family had moved to Johannesburg when Desmond was twelve. He was seventeen years old when the government passed the laws that officially made him a second-class citizen in his own country.

Although Tutu wanted to follow a medical career, his family could not afford the training. So, after graduating from Western High School in Johannesburg, he went to Bantu Normal College in Pretoria, the nation's capital, and then to the University of Johannesburg to become a schoolteacher. During this period he married Leah Nomalizo Shenxane. They would eventually have three daughters and one son.

Tutu's teaching career lasted just three years. When the government, in 1957, set up a "second-class" teaching system for blacks, known as Bantu education, Tutu, along with others, resigned in protest.

Tutu next turned to the study of theology because, as he later said, "God grabbed him by the scruff of the neck." Although he admits his ideals were not so high at the beginning of his religious education, they took root as his training progressed. By his ordination in 1961, he was committed to the Anglican religion. He had converted to that faith because of his admiration for a white priest, Trevor Huddleston, who became his friend and mentor. Huddleston gained a reputation as the leading spokesman in South Africa against racial discrimination. When Tutu spent nearly two years in a hospital recovering from tuberculosis, Huddleston visited the teenager almost every day.

In England during the late 1960s, Tutu earned a master's degree in theology at King's College and later taught at parishes in London and Surrey. For the next few years he lectured in England, Asia, and Africa. His lectures became more and more critical of the racial policies of his homeland. He spoke out against them, aware all the time that in South Africa blacks were becoming increasingly restless and violent. Although Tutu understood their rage and frustration, he was a man of nonviolence—like Gandhi, whom he admired—and remained committed to its principles.

Tutu returned to South Africa in 1975 and became the first black to be named dean of Johannesburg. A year later he was consecrated as bishop of Lesotho. Also in that year he tried to keep angry youths from resorting to violence in the black ghetto township of Soweto, outside of Johannesburg. But when he wrote a letter to South Africa's prime minister to warn him of possible trouble, it was ignored. In the Soweto riots that followed, six hundred blacks were shot to death by government forces.

Tutu's nonviolent stance and his eloquent speeches on the injustice of apartheid began to draw international attention. In 1978 he became the first black secretary-general of the South African Council of Churches, representing some 13 million Christians.

The bishop may have been admired outside of South Africa, but he was not earning raves from his own government. Always touchy about criticism of its treatment of blacks, the government was outraged when Tutu insisted that black South Africans were starving, not through lack of food but through a deliberate government policy. But that was nothing compared to its outrage when Tutu, making a speech in Denmark in 1979, urged other countries to stop trading with his homeland. When he returned to South Africa, his passport was taken away.

But Bishop Tutu would not be silenced. When his passport was returned in 1981, he traveled to the United States and Europe and implored all foreign governments to help stop the dreadful policy of apartheid by refusing to trade with South Africa. Three years later, on another trip to the United States, Tutu learned that he had been awarded the Nobel Peace Prize. His own government, as might be imagined, was silent at the news. Tutu's reaction also might be imagined: "Hey, we are winning! Justice is going to win."

Victory was still a long way off. The United Nations condemned South Africa's racial policy. So did many countries. But discrimination continued, and so did violence. Even the bishop's family was involved. His son Trevor was arrested for protesting a police roundup of schoolchildren. The bishop himself more than once tried to protect those who protested, throwing his slight body—he is only 5 feet 3 inches (160 centimeters)—between them and the police.

Tutu leads the
procession at funeral
services for four anti-
apartheid protesters
who died in clashes
with police.

There is, however, at last hope for peace. In 1989 Frederik W. de Klerk became president and called for talks on a new constitution, involving all races. He lifted restrictions on political organizations such as the African National Congress, whose leader, Nelson Mandela, was freed in 1990 after twenty-seven years in prison. In 1991 de Klerk announced plans to end all apartheid laws. And in 1994 came the first-ever free elections for South Africa. Nelson Mandela became president as head of a multiracial government.

Even a multiracial South African government does not have an untroubled future. The road ahead is difficult, and change is not easy. Many South African blacks are impatient and angry. They fight not only against whites but among themselves. South African blacks may be united in a common cause for freedom but not in how to achieve it or how it should be handled. Many South African whites are defiant. Others are so fearful that they have left their native land to make a life elsewhere.

Tutu has warned his people of the dangers of a bloodbath. In the past this man of peace has been criticized for such words. The old South African government sometimes regarded him as a troublemaker, perhaps even worse. But Desmond Tutu sees himself as a peacemaker, as did the Nobel Peace Prize committee. Although he is well aware of the dangers his country faces, even with reform, he tries increasingly by inspiring actions and words to create a sense of justice, peace, and reconciliation in his homeland.

OSCAR ARIAS SANCHEZ

(1941-   )

PRESIDENT OF COSTA RICA,
1986-1990; WINNER,
1987 NOBEL PEACE PRIZE

"It is for the new generation that we must understand more than ever that peace can only be achieved through its own instruments: dialogue and understanding, tolerance and forgiveness; freedom and democracy."

Those are the words and the feelings of Dr. Oscar Arias Sanchez, former president of Costa Rica and winner of the 1987 Nobel Peace Prize. He has also said, "Weapons do not fire on their own. Those who have lost hope fire them. We must fearlessly fight for peace."

Arias was born into one of Costa Rica's wealthiest coffee-growing families on September 13, 1941. When he was elected president in 1986, he pledged himself and his country to "maintain Costa Rica apart from the Central American armed conflicts. . . . We will struggle by diplomatic and political means, so that in Central America brethren stop killing each other."

A tall order indeed for a country so close to other nations' revolutions, drug wars, bloodshed, and a constant struggle by millions of poor people for a better life. Through all this, the Republic of Costa Rica has never known slavery and did away with the death penalty more than a century ago. It is determined to show the world

(61)

Costa Rican president Oscar Arias Sanchez won regional peace where many efforts had failed.

that "a nation can live in democracy and liberty without armed forces."

How did this peaceful philosophy grow and survive in a land so often surrounded by armed conflict?

Costa Rica is one of seven countries that make up Central America. Belize, El Salvador, Guatemala, Honduras, Nicaragua, and Panama are the others. Central America is a curving neck of land that separates the Pacific Ocean from the Caribbean Sea and connects Mexico—that is, North America—to Colombia on the South American continent.

Costa Rica is a small country: two Costa Ricas could fit into Kentucky. Nicaragua is to the north, Panama to the south. The population numbers about three million, with the largest concentration in and around the capital city of San José.

Columbus's fourth voyage to the New World, in 1502, landed him on the shores of Costa Rica, which means "rich coast" in Spanish. Apparently, Spain didn't find the tiny land rich enough because it was mostly ignored by European invaders until 1564. The Spanish settled Cartago, which was the capital city until the present capital was named in 1823.

Lacking the rich resources of surrounding lands, Costa Rica became a country of small landowners who grew coffee and other crops. They took personal interest in their government and are credited with the country's early growth of democratic ideals. When Mexico declared itself independent from Spain in 1821, Costa Rica joined the Mexican Empire for a short time. Then it helped to create and stayed part of the United Provinces of Central America until 1838, but went its own way thereafter.

Through much of its history, Costa Rica has kept a record of democratic government and orderly elections. But there have been upheavals. One of its most serious was a short experiment with dictatorship in 1917. No one received a majority vote in the election that year, so the assembly chose a president. General Federico Tinoco was unhappy with the choice and led a revolution. Costa Ricans soon grew unhappy with the general's dictatorship, and he was ousted in 1919.

The next crisis occurred in 1948. Some government members, thought to be Communists, tried to prevent the elected president from taking office. Their rebellion was put down, however. A new constitution was passed. It outlawed the army and replaced it with a civil guard.

Since then, Costa Rica's internal troubles have been mainly economic. However, Arias had to spend most of his years in office trying to end the bitter struggles in the neighboring countries of El Salvador, Nicaragua, and Guatemala. In doing so, he became a man noted for his dedication to peace and did more than any other to reduce tensions in Central America during this period.

Well educated and trained, Arias Sanchez worked to ease his country's money woes and to guide it politically through troubled times. He studied economics at the University of Costa Rica and earned a master's degree and a doctorate in political science from the University of Essex in England.

For a short time, 1969–1972, Arias taught political science at the University of Costa Rica. He married Margarita Penón Góngora, a biochemist, in 1973. They have two children, Sylvia and Oscar Felipe.

In the 1960s Arias had begun working for the moderate National Liberation party (PLN). He became the party's secretary-general in 1979 and was elected the country's president in 1986.

Arias immediately took measures to try to ease Costa Rica's staggering economic problems, such as an awesome foreign debt. And he worked tirelessly to restore peace and political stability to other Central American countries. Neighboring Nicaragua was heavily involved in bitter fighting between the government, led by the leftist Sandinista party, and guerrilla opponents, known as contras. Although Arias was very critical of the government, he would not allow the contras to operate militarily on Costa Rican soil. Civil war also raged in El Salvador, and rebellion broke out repeatedly in Honduras. Both countries were ruled by right-wing governments.

In 1987 Arias was the main force in setting up a regional peace plan for Central America. It set dates for cease-fires and for demo-

Central American leaders at a summit meeting early in 1988. From left are José Azcona of Honduras, José Napoleon Duarte of El Salvador, Arias, Vinicio Cerezo of Guatemala, and Daniel Ortega of Nicaragua.

cratic elections. It was signed by Arias and the leaders of Guatemala, El Salvador, Honduras, and Nicaragua.

In recognition of his work to bring peace to the region, Dr. Arias Sanchez was awarded the Nobel Peace Prize in 1987. In his acceptance speech in Oslo, Norway, he said:

> To receive this Nobel Prize on the 10th of December is for me a marvelous coincidence. My son Oscar Felipe, here present, is eight years old today. I say to him, and through him to all the children of my country, that we shall never resort to violence, we shall never support military solutions to the problems of Central America.

Costa Rican law limits a president to just one term. Since leaving office, Arias has traveled to all parts of the world to bring his message of peace. He is proud of the message and proud of his country: "Mine is an unarmed people whose children have never seen a fighter or a tank or a warship." And he adds with greater pride, "My country is a country of teachers. It is therefore a country of peace. . . . Our children go about with books under their arms, not with rifles on their shoulders."

In his own country and in countries around the world, Oscar Arias Sanchez is a seeker of peace who practices what he preaches. "Peace," he says, "is not only a matter of noble words."

BETTY WILLIAMS
(1943-)

MAIREAD CORRIGAN MAGUIRE
(1944-)

PEACE PEOPLE OF
NORTHERN IRELAND; WINNERS,
1976 NOBEL PEACE PRIZE

Although the cause they began is far from won, these two women fought for peace in a land that seems to have lost itself in violence.

To begin to understand the bitterness and hatred that are tearing apart Northern Ireland, it is first necessary to understand where this country is and why it is. Northern Ireland is made up of six counties in the northeast corner of Ireland, an island slightly larger than the state of West Virginia. It sits in the Atlantic Ocean off Great Britain's western coast. Most of the island is occupied by the independent Republic of Ireland with its capital at Dublin. Northern Ireland, with its capital at Belfast, is part of the United Kingdom along with England, Wales, and Scotland.

For many centuries, all of the island was part of the United Kingdom. But the Irish, in the southern counties especially, demanded independence. They periodically, and often violently, rebelled against British authority. Finally, in 1921, the British agreed to free Ireland, but they retained the six counties of Northern Ireland. In 1948 Ireland withdrew from the British Commonwealth of Nations.

Almost all of Ireland's population is Catholic. Northern Ireland, also known as Ulster, has about one and a half million people. Two thirds of them are Protestant, the rest Catholic. The minority Catholics felt they were second-class citizens. They wanted to be part of the Republic of Ireland. Although it seems at first glance that the violence in Northern Ireland is solely over religious beliefs, it goes beyond that. Catholics have long believed that they have been ignored under the rule of Great Britain, a Protestant country. They argue that Protestants get better jobs and higher positions in government, and have higher social status than Catholics.

Over the years, bitterness has turned to unrest and unrest has turned to hatred. The country erupted in violent protests in the 1960s, and the fighting has been going on ever since with no end in sight. Even as the number of deaths declines, the incidents grow more deadly. The Irish Republican Army (IRA), which is Catholic, and the Ulster Defense Association, Protestant, are only two of the many groups that place bombs in buildings and assassinate leaders. Innocent men, women, and children die in the streets of Belfast and London and elsewhere. British soldiers are sent into Northern Ireland to bring order. They shoot and kill and are shot at and killed. The situation has become so senseless that just to walk into the wrong neighborhood in Belfast is to risk death. The streets of the city are walled off to keep Catholic neighbor from Protestant neighbor.

Between 1968 and 1976 more than 1,600 people died from this hatred in Northern Ireland. Counted among the dead of that period were three children of the Maguire family, ages eight, two and a half, and six weeks. On August 10, 1976, a lovely summer day, Anne Maguire decided to take a walk in Belfast with three of her children. They walked into the middle of a fight between the IRA and the British Army. The children were killed, and Anne was badly wounded. Until her death in January 1980 she never completely recovered, physically or emotionally, from the trauma.

Two other women of Northern Ireland also never completely recovered from that tragedy. One saw it happen. She is Betty Smyth Williams, a tough, outspoken, relentless fighter for peace.

Betty Williams (left) and Mairead Corrigan read an oath of peace at a rally in Northern Ireland in 1976. Their commitment to peace pushed them into the international spotlight.

Betty Smyth was born in a Catholic section of Belfast on May 22, 1943. Ironically, her mother, a waitress, was Catholic and her father, a butcher, Protestant. Her mother was paralyzed by a stroke when Betty was thirteen, and the young girl took over the care of her younger sister, Margaret. Their father tried to raise the girls to be without prejudice, a not so easy task in Northern Ireland.

In 1961 Betty married an Englishman and a Protestant, Ralph Edward Williams. They would eventually have two children, Deborah and Paul. Because Ralph was an engineer with the Merchant Marine, Betty traveled to various places with her husband, including New York City.

Back in Northern Ireland, Betty Williams at first sympathized with the aims of the IRA to cut the ties between Britain and Northern Ireland. But when the IRA resorted to bombings, shootings, and other violence, she withdrew her support. In 1972 she joined a peaceful protest called Witness for Peace, led by a Protestant clergyman, in an effort to bring Catholics and Protestants together. The following year she tried to comfort a young British soldier as he lay dying of a gunshot wound in a Belfast street. Other women nearby yelled at her for aiding a Protestant. Later she said of that incident, "I learned that people had obviously lost their sense of value of human life."

In 1976 Williams witnessed another horror when Anne Maguire and her children were struck down. It brought her in contact with the woman who would share the 1976 Nobel Peace Prize with her, Mairead Corrigan Maguire. Mairead too would never completely recover from the tragedy of the Maguire family, for Anne Maguire was her sister.

Mairead Corrigan was also born in Belfast, on January 27, 1944, the second of seven children in a Catholic family. Her father, a window cleaner, could not afford to send her to school beyond age fourteen. She worked as a baby-sitter to earn the money for business school, at sixteen got her first job as an assistant bookkeeper, and at twenty-one was a secretary in a brewery. Eventually, she rose to become private secretary to one of the firm's directors.

She remembers growing up with a fear of the IRA and a hatred of British soldiers. She did volunteer work with a Catholic welfare organization, the Legion of Mary. As she said later, "I was pretty much the typical young Catholic from the Catholic ghetto."

Although Mairead Corrigan was well aware of the growing dissension in her country and sympathetic toward the views of many Catholics about second-class citizenship, she did not come face-to-face with violence until the early 1970s. When she watched the first burning of Catholics' houses and the revenge against Protestants, she was horrified. Her horror grew far stronger in 1976 when her sister's children were killed on a Belfast street.

The day after the tragedy, gentle, soft-spoken Mairead Corrigan appeared on television and tearfully pleaded for an end to the madness. She also blamed the IRA for the killings, something unheard of for a Roman Catholic.

Betty Williams saw the television plea. Mairead Corrigan's courage only increased her own anger over the tragedy. Within hours she was knocking on doors in Belfast—a dangerous activity in itself—and asking people to sign a petition for peace. Within two days she had six thousand signatures. Williams also went on television asking all Irish women, Protestant and Catholic, to pressure the IRA to stop the violence.

In response, Mairead Corrigan asked Betty Williams to attend the funeral of the Maguire children. The two women peace fighters met and combined forces. On August 14 approximately ten thousand women responded to their call for a peaceful demonstration. With Williams and Corrigan in the lead, they bravely marched to the gravesite of the Maguire children to pray and sing hymns. On the way they were physically and verbally assaulted by IRA members and sympathizers.

But it was too late now to stop these two determined peace fighters. They formed what was first called Women for Peace. By the end of August they had held three peace marches and gained thirty thousand followers.

In their efforts, Williams and Corrigan were greatly aided by Ciaran McKeown, a reporter for the *Irish Press*. Said McKeown, "We talked, and we formed a kind of agreement to trust each other. . . . Just by looking at them, I knew I could count on them." His knowledge of Northern Ireland politics and his newspaper background were great assets in their plans for a peace movement, which McKeown suggested be called Community of Peace People.

All during the autumn of 1976 the Peace People movement gathered momentum. Small peace groups were established all over Northern Ireland. Rallies and marches drew large, quiet crowds. McKeown published a pamphlet called *The Price of Peace*, about peace and nonviolence. Williams and Corrigan started a magazine called *Peace by Peace*. They organized peace walks and helped to arrange escapes for those whom terrorists had marked for death. They used the media where and when they could to carry their message.

Corrigan left her job at the brewery, and the two women began drawing small salaries from the movement. They also began to take their message outside of Northern Ireland. The Peace People drew attention in other parts of the world. Financial aid came in from such places as Australia and New Zealand, Canada, and Mexico. American folk singer Joan Baez joined the women at a rally in London. U.S. president Jimmy Carter urged the American people not to give money to the terrorists. Williams and Corrigan themselves visited the United States in 1976 to advise against donating money to any organization that favored violence in Northern Ireland.

For their tireless work and energy in the cause, Williams and Corrigan seemed to be the obvious choices to win the 1976 Nobel Peace Prize. It can be awarded yearly to the person, institution, or organization judged to have done the most to bring peace to the world. However, the Nobel committee had a problem. The deadline for Peace Prize nominations is February 1, and that was long past. So, Williams and Corrigan were not eligible to win. Yet the Peace Prize committee does not have to nominate anyone in a given year if they cannot find a worthy candidate. The committee decided that none was as worthy as the Peace People.

In November the two women traveled to Oslo, Norway, where the Nobel Peace Prize is awarded. They were given a special Norwegian People's Peace Prize, along with private donations of $340,000 collected in Norway. Williams and Corrigan vowed to spend the money on expanding their movement.

The following year, in October 1977, Betty Williams and Mairead Corrigan were belatedly awarded the 1976 Nobel Peace Prize. The 1977 winner was the organization known as Amnesty International. The Peace People were the first women to receive the prize since 1944, when U.S. cowinner Emily G. Balch, an economist and pacifist, won for her "promotion of peace in the world." Williams and Corrigan shared part of their $140,000 prize money with Ciaran McKeown.

The prize money allowed them to buy a small headquarters building for the peace movement and to start up some local chapters. Then the two women took themselves off the payroll of the Peace People organization and continued to work, as volunteers.

Williams and Corrigan have received other recognition besides the Peace Prize, such as honorary doctorates from Yale University and an invitation to visit Queen Elizabeth II. But not everyone admires the peace women of Northern Ireland. Groups on both sides, Catholic and Protestant, have called them traitors to their country. Threats on their lives have not been uncommon. "Shoot Betty" signs have often appeared on Belfast walls. Betty Williams is by far the more vocal of the two women. Comparing her more soft-spoken, emotional partner to herself, Williams said, "They call us the saint and the sinner."

Other critics have said that the Peace People and their movement are naïve, that the only ones who can stop the fighting are the ones who are doing it: the IRA, the British Army, and Protestant groups. However, the killings and violence did decline somewhat in the following years, and some of the credit must go to the efforts of these two women of Northern Ireland.

Once, when challenged with the fact that the movement had not brought peace, Williams answered that it had "created a climate for peace to become respectable." Perhaps only the years ahead will tell if that is so. Sometimes there seems some hope for real change. In June 1991 Northern Ireland's four main political parties met in Belfast for roundtable talks. No agreement was reached, but it was the first time that the four had talked at all in sixteen years. That in itself was hopeful.

Yet the violence continues. Early in 1991 the IRA bombed the British prime minister's home at 10 Downing Street in London. Nearly two weeks later an IRA bomb exploded at a London railway station, killing one and injuring many. That November an IRA bomb damaged a hospital in Belfast and injured a number of children. In May 1993 two children were killed by a bomb blast in England.

Where does the madness end? When and how?

Although Williams and Corrigan now leave the direct operation of the Peace People movement to others, they still passionately believe in the cause. In late 1981 Mairead Corrigan married Jackie Maguire, widower of her sister Anne. Besides her dead sister's remaining children, the Maguires now have two sons of their own, John Francis and Luke.

When Luke, born in 1984, was still a toddler, Mairead Maguire wrote *A Letter to My Son Luke* in the form of a pamphlet printed by the Peace People movement. It said in part:

> . . . you too must give "justice" and respect every person's right to life. This means, my little son, that you must never kill another human being. . . . It will not be easy for you to refuse to kill. Sadly we live in a world where those who refuse to kill and choose to live nonviolent lives are looked on as naïve or as cowards. . . . Remember, Luke, you have no country. The world is your country. You have not only two brothers and two sisters but millions of brothers and sisters.

CONCLUSION

*P*eople of Peace is the story of a small number of people who have worked for and are working at the same enormous task—peace on earth. There have been many others; there will be many more who join hands in a large circle around the globe. From the United States to Latin America, to Europe, Asia, Africa, the Middle East, and everywhere, people are dedicating their lives and their work to bringing peace to their nations and to every land.

President Jimmy Carter's Conflict Resolution Program of the Carter Center is just one organization in which caring people band together and work toward peace. Amnesty International, headquartered in London, is especially concerned with freeing political prisoners. It tries to make sure that people who work for world harmony do not die fighting against violence. Organizations, clubs, and centers in all countries, each in its own way, try to bring peace to their own small part of the world.

In Costa Rica, Oscar Arias Sanchez told his son that we must not use weapons. In Northern Ireland, Mairead Corrigan Maguire wrote to her young son that little children must not grow up to kill each other. From South Africa, from India, from the United Nations, and from the United States, the message is the same. And it is clear. War must not be the way to settle differences. The people of the world must find another answer so that all can live out their lives without fear, and children can live with hope for the future.

The eleven people of peace in this book were and are dedicated. But they are not enough, for the world we live in is still far from peaceful. Perhaps, however, they will serve as examples of what can happen if everyone decides to follow their path of hard work and caring.

Our *People of Peace* have shared the work for their cause. They have spread the word that war is bad for children and for everyone. Like balloons heading upward for all to see, they have sent to the world a message of

PEACE.

A PEACE GLOSSARY

apartheid — a policy of racial segregation carried out in South Africa until the 1990s

bigotry — intolerance of another's race, religion, or sex

incumbent — a person who holds a public office

mediator — a person who tries to settle a dispute between opposing parties

militant — a person engaged in warfare, or who is aggressively active in a cause

pacifist — a person opposed to violence as a means to settle a dispute

partition — division or separation

philanthropist — a person who promotes human welfare by generous acts or gifts

tycoon — a powerful businessperson

FOR FURTHER READING

Aaseng, Nathan. *The Peace Seekers: The Nobel Peace Prize.* Minneapolis: Lerner, 1987.

Bowman, John. *Andrew Carnegie.* Morristown, N.J.: Silver Burdett, 1989.

Carter, Jimmy. *Talking Peace: A Vision for the Next Generation.* New York: Dutton, 1993.

Jacobs, William Jay. *Great Lives: Human Rights.* New York: Scribner, 1990.

McKissack, Patricia, and Fredrick McKissack. *Ralphe J. Bunche: Peacemaker.* Hillside, N.J.: Enslow, 1991.

Meyer, Caroline. *Voices of Northern Ireland: Growing Up in a Troubled Land.* San Diego: Harcourt Brace, 1992.

Mitchard, Jacqueline. *Jane Addams: Pioneer in Social Reform and Activist for World Peace.* Milwaukee: Gareth Stevens, 1991.

Peduzzi, Kelli, and Ronnie Cummins. *Oscar Arias: Peacemaker and Leader Among Nations.* Milwaukee: Gareth Stevens, 1991.

Randolph, Sallie. *Woodrow Wilson.* New York: Walker, 1992.

Sheldon, Richard. *Dag Hammarskjold.* New York: Chelsea House, 1987.

Sherrow, Victoria. *Mohandas Gandhi: The Power of the Spirit.* The Millbrook Press, 1994.

Wade, Linda R. *James Carter.* Chicago: Childrens Press, 1989.

Wimer, David. *Desmond Tutu: Religious Leader Devoted to Freedom.* Milwaukee: Gareth Stevens, 1991.

INDEX